DOMINICK ARGENTO
WALDEN POND

Nocturnes and Barcarolles
For Mixed Chorus,
Three Violoncellos and Harp

Full Score

BOOSEY & HAWKES

AN IMAGEM COMPANY

DISTRIBUTED BY

HAL•LEONARD®
CORPORATION
7777 W. BLUEMOUND RD. P.O. BOX 13819 MILWAUKEE, WI 53213

www.boosey.com
www.halleonard.com

Published by Boosey & Hawkes, Inc.
229 West 28th Street, 11th Floor
New York NY 10001

www.boosey.com

 AN IMAGEM COMPANY

ISMN 979-0-051-26170-3

Commissioned by and dedicated to
Dale Warland and The Dale Warland Singers
on the occasion of their 25th anniversary

Commissioned also, in part, by
The Barlow Endowment for Music Composition at
Brigham Young University

First performed on October 26, 1996 at the
Ted Mann Concert Hall, Minneapolis, Minnesota
by The Dale Warland Singers
conducted by Dale Warland

First recorded by the
Dale Warland Singers
conducted by Dale Warland on
Gothic Records G 49217

Choral Score (ISMN 979-0-051-47525-4) and Parts (ISMN 979-0-051-10509-0)

are available separately for sale through Hal Leonard

CONTENTS

Duration: *ca.* 25 minutes

TEXT BY HENRY DAVID THOREAU
FROM *WALDEN*

I. THE POND

Nothing so fair, so pure lies on the surface of the earth. It is a clear and deep green well, half a mile long, a perennial spring in the midst of pine and oak woods.

It is earth's eye; looking into which the beholder measures the depth of his own nature; it is a mirror which no stone can crack, whose quicksilver will never wear off; a mirror which retains no breath that is breathed on it, but sends its own to float as clouds high above its surface, and be reflected on its bosom still.

There are few traces of man's hand to be seen. The water laves the shore as it did a thousand years ago. This water is of such crystalline purity that the body of the bather appears of an alabaster whiteness, which, as the limbs are magnified and distorted, produces a monstrous effect, making fit studies for Michael Angelo.

So pure, so fair.

II. ANGLING

In warm evenings I frequently sat in the boat playing the flute, and saw the perch, which I seem to have charmed, hovering around me, and the moon travelling over the ribbed bottom, which was strewed with the wrecks of the forest.

Sometimes, I spent the hours of midnight fishing from a boat anchored in forty feet of water and communicating by a long flaxen line with mysterious nocturnal fishes, serenaded by owls and foxes, and hearing, from time to time, the creaking note of some unknown bird close at hand.

There was one older man, an excellent fisher; once in a while we sat together on the pond, he at one end of the boat, and I at the other; but not many words passed between us, for he had grown deaf in his later years, but he occasionally hummed a psalm, which harmonized well enough with my philosophy. Our intercourse was thus altogether one of unbroken harmony, far more pleasing to remember than if it had been carried on by speech.

III. OBSERVING

It is a soothing employment to sit on a stump, on a height over-looking the pond, and study the dimpling circles incessantly inscribed on its surface amid the reflected skies and trees.

It may be that in the distance a fish describes an arc of three or four feet in the air, and there is one bright flash where it emerges, and another where it strikes the water. Or here and there, a pickerel or shiner picks an insect from this smooth surface; it is wonderful with what elaborateness this simple fact is advertised—this piscine murder will out—reported in circling dimples, in lines of beauty, the constant welling up of its fountain, the gentle pulsing of its life, the heaving of its breast. Then the trembling circles seek the shore and all is smooth again. One November afternoon, the pond was remarkably smooth, so that it was difficult to distinguish its surface. I was surprised to find myself surrounded by myriads of small, bronze-colored perch. In such transparent water, reflecting the clouds, I seemed to be floating through the air as in a balloon, and their swimming impressed me as a kind of flight or hovering, as if they were birds passing just beneath my level, their fins, like sails, set all around them.

IV. EXTOLLING

Sky water.

Lake of light.

Great crystal on the surface of the earth.

Successive nations perchance have drank at, admired, and fathomed it, and passed away, and still its water is green and pellucid as ever. Who knows in how many unremembered nations' literatures this has been the Castalian Fountain? or what nymphs presided over it in the Golden Age?

Perhaps on that spring morning when Adam and Eve were driven out of Eden Walden Pond was already in existence, and even then breaking up in a gentle spring rain and covered with ducks and geese, which had not heard of the fall. Even then it had clarified its waters and colored them of the hue they now wear, and obtained a patent of Heaven to be the only Walden Pond in the world.

V. WALDEN REVISITED

Since I left those shores the wood-choppers have laid them waste, but I remember, I remember...

I remember when I first paddled a boat on Walden, it was completely surrounded by thick and lofty pine and oak woods, and in some of its coves grape-vines had run over the trees next the water and formed bowers under which a boat could pass. I have spent many an hour floating over its surface as the zephyr willed, in a summer fore-noon, lying on my back across the seats, dreaming awake.

And though the woodchoppers have laid bare first this shore and then that, it struck me again tonight, —Why, here is Walden, the same woodland lake that I discovered so many years ago; where a forest was cut down last winter another is springing up as lustily as ever; the same thought is welling up to its surface that was then; it is the same liquid joy and happiness to itself and its Maker. He rounded this water with his hand, deepened and clarified it in his thought. I see by its face that it is visited by the same reflection; and I can almost say,

Walden, is it you?

WALDEN POND

I. The Pond

HENRY DAVID THOREAU

DOMINICK ARGENTO

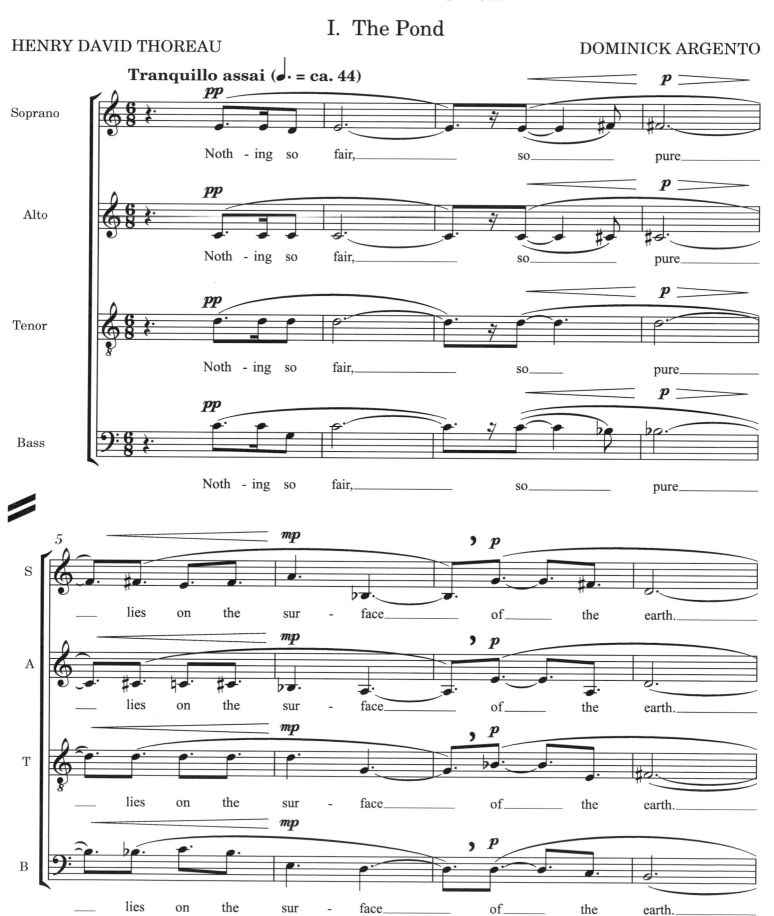

979-0-051-26170-3

Printed in U.S.A.

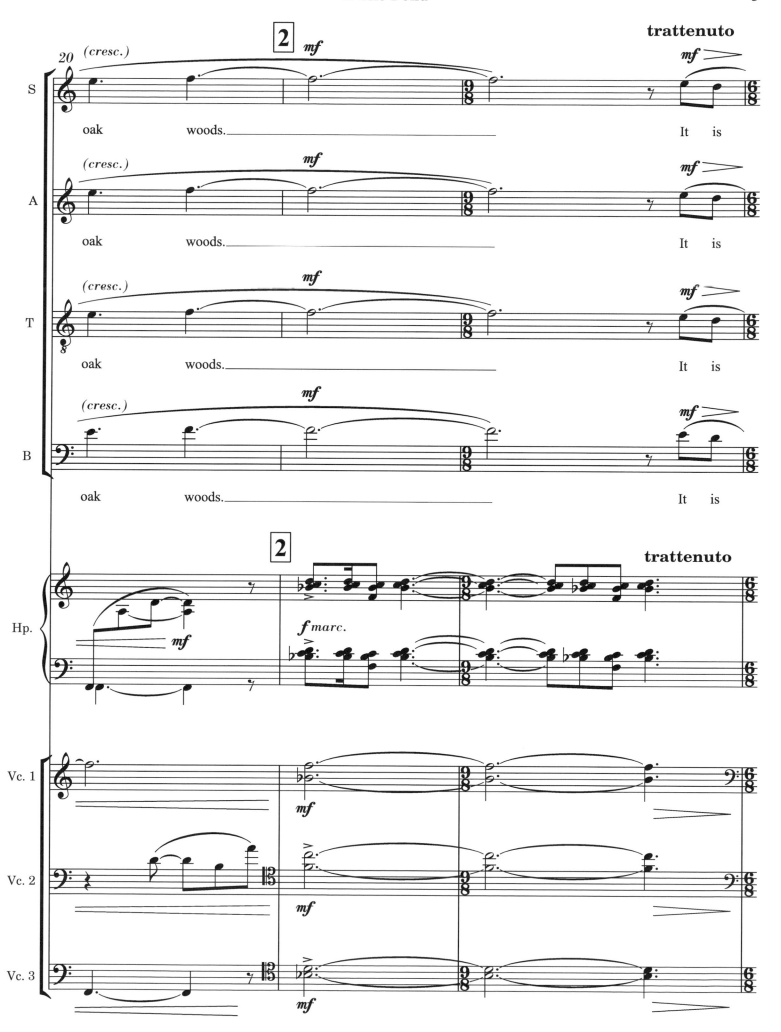

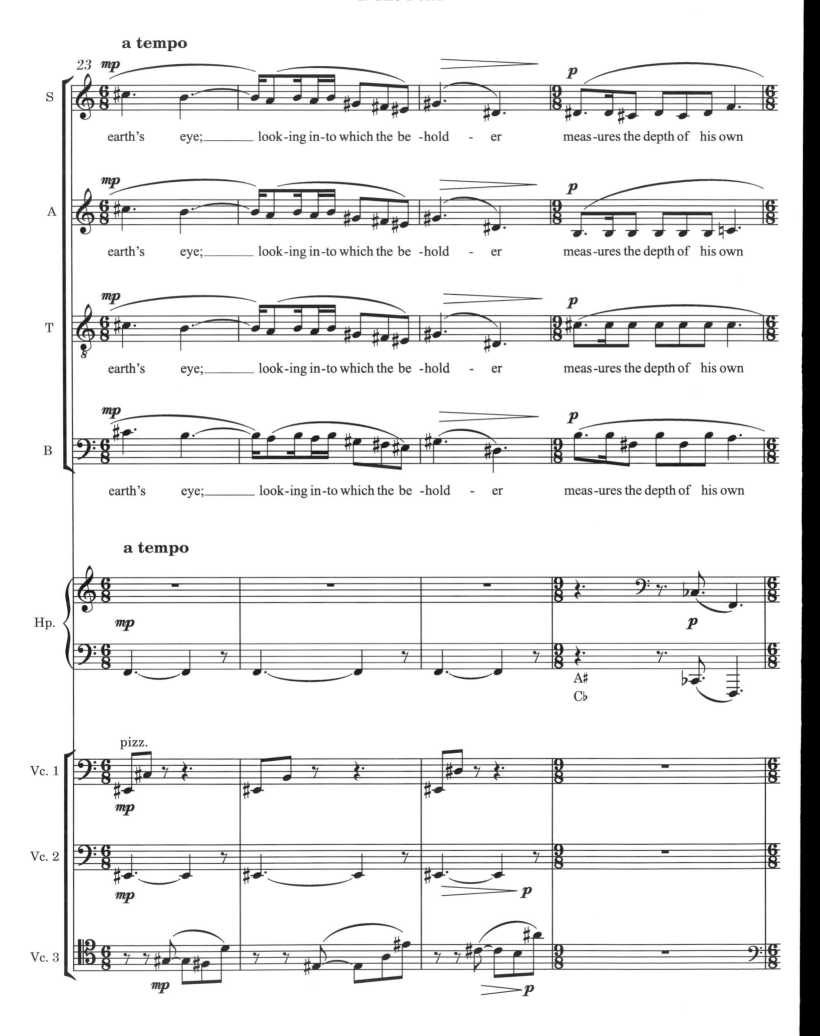

II. Angling

*Continue playing as harmonics (natural or artificial) until 11 .

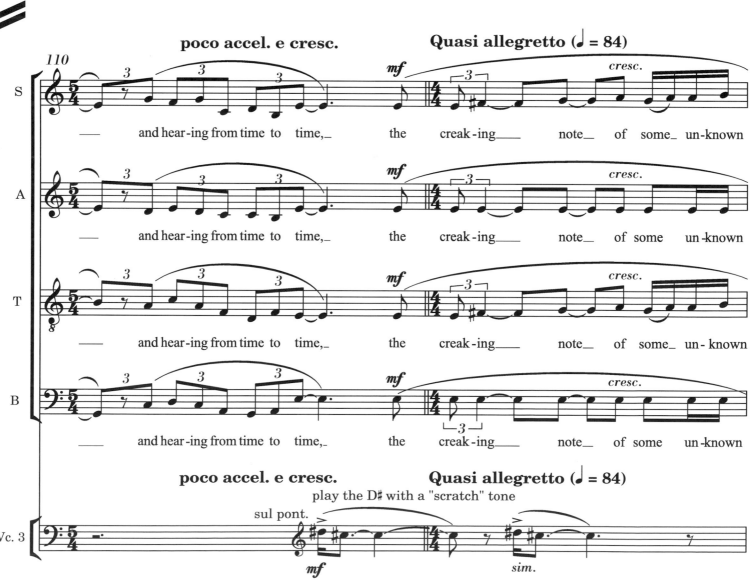

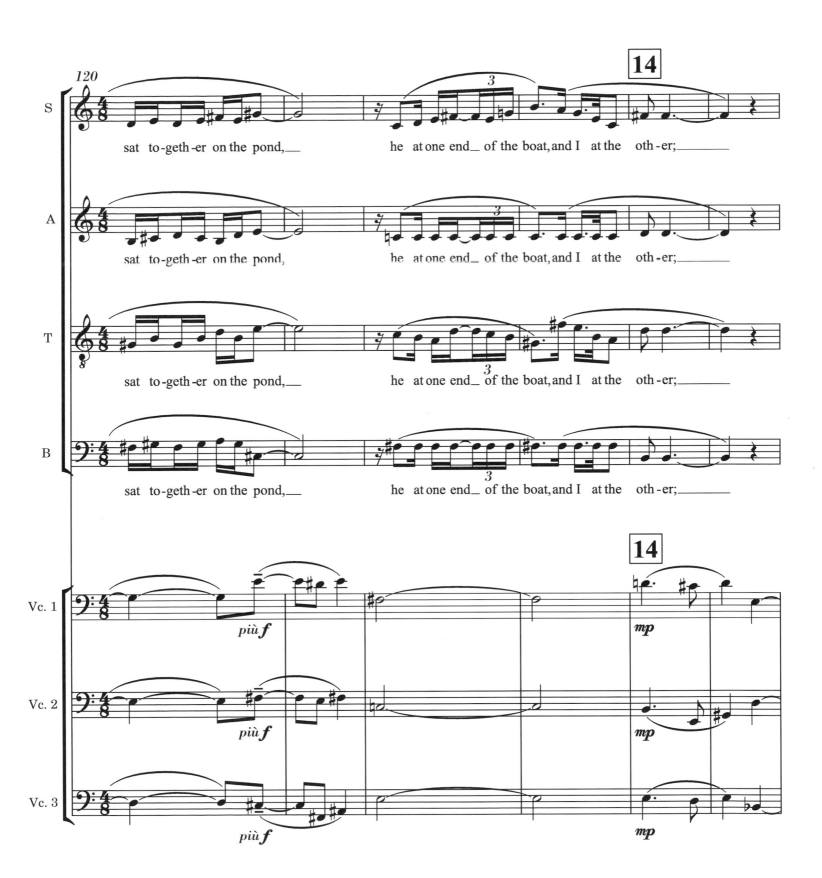

but not man-y words passed be-tween us,————— for he had grown deaf in his la-ter years,

15 **Stesso tempo**

136

S: los - o - phy.___   Our   in - ter - course was thus al - to-geth -er   one

A: los - o - phy.___   Our   in - ter - course was thus al - to-geth -er   one

T: (hum)___

B: los - o - phy.___   Our   in - ter - course was thus al - to-geth -er   one

139

S: ___ of un-brok -en har-mo -ny,___   far   more pleas -ing to re -

A: ___ of un-brok -en har-mo -ny,___   far   more pleas -ing to re -

T: ___ (hum)___

B: ___ of un-brok -en har-mo -ny,___   far   more pleas-ing to re -

III. Observing

Stesso movimento (♩ = ♩. del prec.)

cresc.   f

mp

S

It may be___ that in the dis-tance___ a fish de-scribes an arc of three or four feet in the air,___

cresc.   f

mp

A

It may be___ that in the dis-tance___ a fish de-scribes an arc of three or four feet in the air,___

gliss.

Hp.

f   Eb F♮ G# Ab
     Bb C♮ D#

brillante sffz

Stesso movimento (♩ = ♩. del prec.)

Vc. 1

fp

Vc. 2

fp

Vc. 3

fp

S

and there is one bright flash___ where it e - mer - ges,___

A

and there is one bright flash___ where it e - mer - ges,___

T

and there is one bright flash___ where it e - mer - ges,___

B

and there is one bright flash___ where it e - mer - ges,___

S: and an -oth - er where it strikes the wa - ter;

A: and an -oth - er where it strikes the wa - ter;

T: and an -oth - er where it strikes the wa - ter;

B: and an -oth - er where it strikes the wa - ter;

Largo misterioso (♩. = ca. 46)

S: or here and there, a pick-er-el or shin-er___ picks an in-sect from this smooth

A: or here and there, a pick-er-el or shin-er___ picks an in-sect from this smooth

T: or here and there, a pick-er-el or shin-er___ picks an in-sect from this smooth

B: or here and there, a pick-er-el or shin-er___ picks an in-sect from this smooth

Largo misterioso (♩. = ca. 46)

IV. Extolling

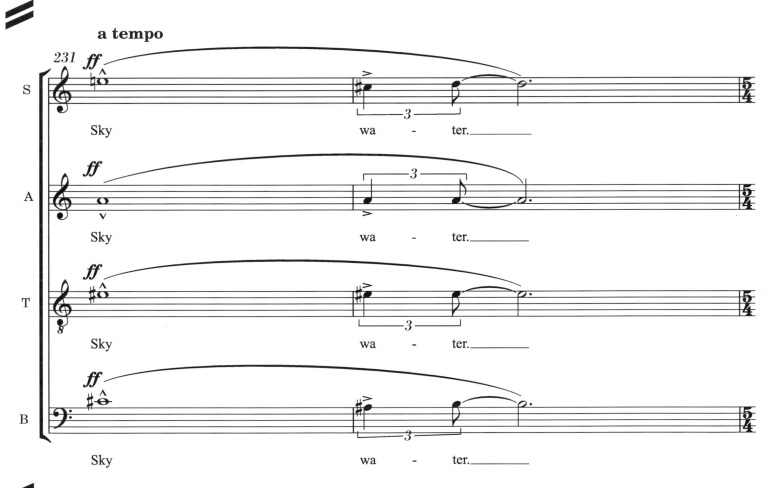

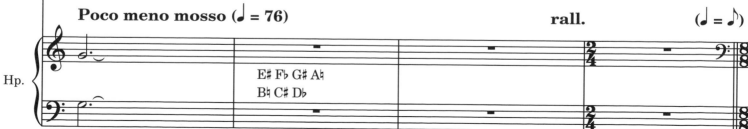

Wal - den Pond_____ was al - read - y_____ in_____ ex -

V. Walden Revisited

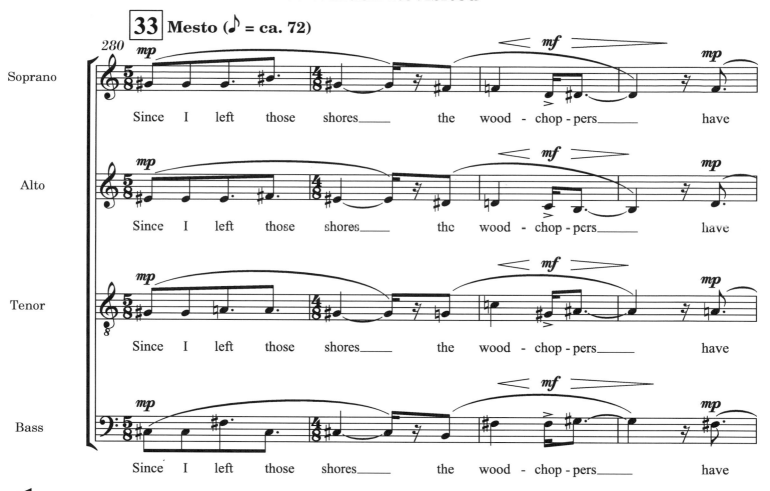

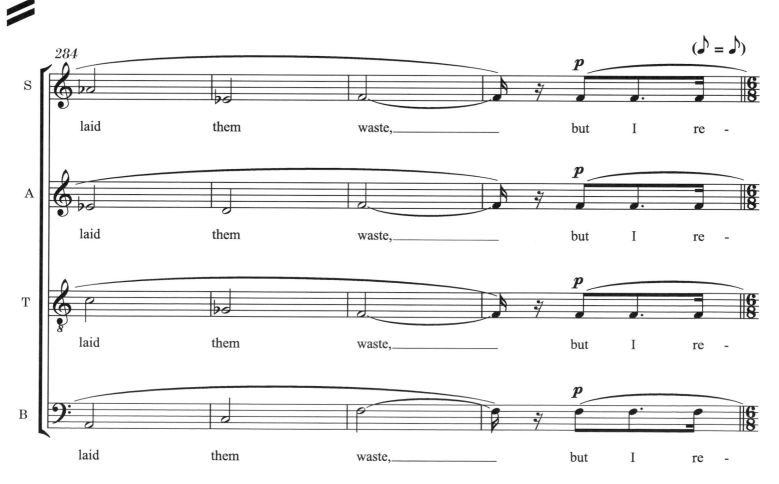

39 **Maestoso** (♪ = ca. 76), **diminuendo poco a poco al fine**

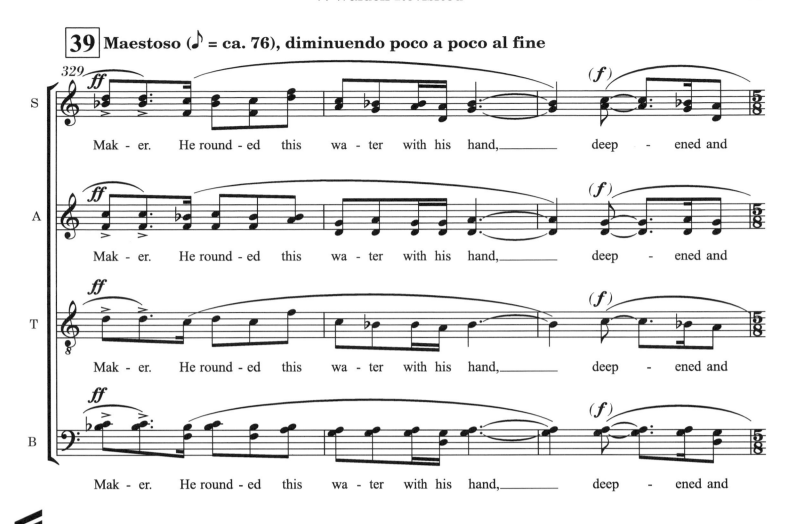

Mak - er. He round - ed this wa - ter with his hand, deep - ened and

clar - i - fied it in his thought, I see by its face that it is

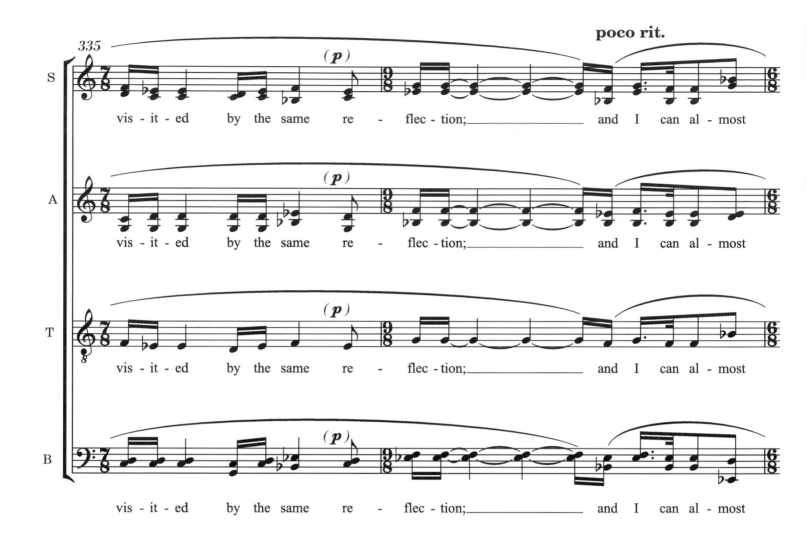